STAFFO MOOR

By Cathryn Walton

Photography by Mark Titterton

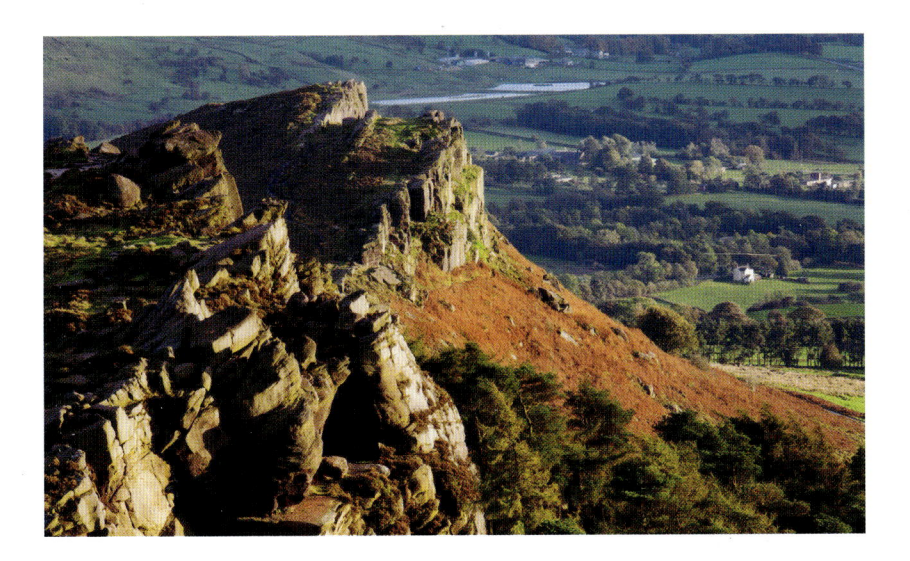

INTRODUCTION

Welcome to the Staffordshire Moorlands where you'll find moors carpeted with purple heather, rolling hills waiting to be walked, paths and tracks to explore and wildlife to be discovered. Have fun at Alton Towers, try a water sport, travel on a steam train, picnic amidst breathtakingly beautiful countryside or simply relax in picturesque villages. A wealth of heritage can be found in our moorland towns, Leek has a French connection, an eighteenth century working corn mill, a sensational silk history and a unique Arts and Crafts heritage. Cheadle cherishes Pugin's Gem and Biddulph boasts a beautiful historic garden. Additionally, a large part of the Peak District National Park is contained within the Staffordshire Moorlands.

ABOVE: The Roaches

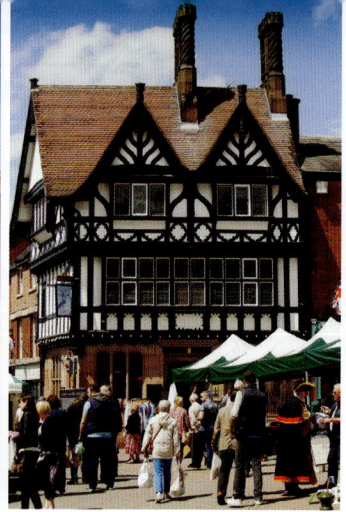

LEEK

Leek has been a thriving market town for centuries and still has weekly markets on Wednesdays and Saturdays as well as monthly Sunday markets.

The 17th century Market Cross still stands in Leek's historic cobbled Market Place. There's so much to see in the Market Place including the Red Lion, a former coaching inn, which started life in the early 1600s as the home of a wealthy mercer, the Victorian Butter Market, the Georgian house, now an Arts Centre, and the Bird in Hand, with its impressive Sugden barley twist chimneys. Nearby St Edward Street has Georgian town houses, once the homes of prominent silk manufacturers.

Don't miss the Nicholson War Memorial one of the largest in the country. The memorial was certainly unusual at the time it was built having been paid for by Arthur Nicholson, a silk manufacturer, who had lost his son, Basil, during WWI. Most memorials were generally paid for by public donations at the time. The memorial is open for guided tours each month. Pick up the self-guided Architectural Trail from the Tourist Information Centre to explore more amazing architecture.

TOP LEFT & MIDDLE: Market Place **RIGHT:** Nicholson War Memorial
ABOVE: The Foxlowe Arts Centre, Church Street

Silk Industry

Leek was an important silk town. The industry began as early as 1672 and by the late 18th century was trading in silk, nationally and internationally on a considerable scale. At first the silk industry was domestic with women and girls sewing silk thread in intricate patterns around button moulds and hand loom weavers working on the top floors of terraced houses. These houses can still be seen in the town, notably in King Street. Later the industry became concentrated in mills which still survive, now converted into apartments, testament to a once thriving industry.

Sugden & Son

Dominating the town is the inspiring architecture of William and Larner Sugden. William came to Leek, in the 1840s, to supervise the building of the stations on the Churnet Valley Railway. He settled in Leek designing many public buildings, shops and houses. His son, Larner, influenced by William Morris, designed many buildings in an Arts and Crafts style, often incorporating sunflowers, terracotta tiles and fancy brickwork into the design. Perhaps Larner Sugden's most imposing building in Leek is the Nicholson Institute in Stockwell Street. Designed in a Queen Ann style, in 1884, it was given to the town by Joshua Nicholson, a wealthy silk manufacturer, who wanted to provide Leek people with a place where they could access art and literature. When built, it provided a library, a museum and an art gallery and still does so today. It's free to enter and well worth a visit to admire the architecture and the changing displays in the museum and art gallery.

TOP: Cross Street Mills **MIDDLE:** Derby Street **BOTTOM:** Nicholson Institute

THE ARTS AND CRAFTS CONNECTION

Leek has unique connections with influential designers and celebrated architects. William Morris, the most influential designer of the 19th century, stayed in Leek several times, from 1875 to 1877, while working on natural dyes with Thomas Wardle. Stroll around Leek and feast your eyes on tiles by William De Morgan, sculpture by Stephen Webb, plaster work by Abraham Broadbent, stained glass by Edward Burne-Jones and Morris & Co, wall paintings by Gerald Horsley and exquisite silk altar cloths designed by John Sedding, Norman Shaw and G G Scott junior. The altar clothes were stitched by the renowned Leek Embroidery Society. Walter Crane worked in Leek and was the first president of the Nicholson Institute.

Norman Shaw, Edmund Street and G F Bodley all worked on Leek churches and All Saints Church on Compton was decorated by members of the Arts and Crafts movement.

RUDYARD

Picturesque Rudyard Lake lies near Leek off the A523. It was constructed in 1797 as a reservoir to supply water to the Caldon Canal and still does so today. These days the lake is a major centre for diverse leisure activities. Fishing, canoeing, sailing, rowing and cycling are all catered for. Hire a boat or board the trip boat 'Honey'. Stroll along the dam head enjoying wonderful views of the lake or visit the exhibitions in two converted boathouses. One provides touch screen facilities to explore the village while the recently restored 'Earl of Macclesfield's boathouse', the oldest boathouse, features the lake's boating history. A pleasant 5 mile walk, through glorious

TOP: Stained glass by Edward-Burne Jones **MIDDLE:** Plaster work by Abraham Broadbent
BOTTOM: Rudyard Lake

countryside, will take you round the lake. Alternatively take the train and travel on the miniature railway which runs alongside the lake. Drinks and snacks are available at the Activity Centre with its outside seating area while the nearby Lake Hotel provides more substantial meals. John Lockwood Kipling and his fiancé were so impressed by Rudyard Lake with its stunning views across the water that they named their first son, Rudyard. Don't miss the remarkable wooden sculpture depicting tightrope walks across the lake.

CHEADLE

Cheadle is an historic market town, the market place has an impressive Georgian stepped wall and a late Georgian terrace with bow windows. Two iron Georgian verandas can be seen in the restored Victorian market hall; they used to stand either side of the Market Place. High Street has an eclectic range of buildings including 16th century timber framed buildings, former Georgian town houses and the 19th century Lulworth House. Cheadle Discovery and Visitor Centre now occupies Lulworth House, offering displays, guided tours and events.

Be sure to visit St Giles Catholic Church, known locally as Pugin's Gem, it's one of the finest examples of Gothic Revival architecture in the country. It has a stunning, elaborately decorated, colourful interior. This beautiful church was designed and built by Augustus W N Pugin, a protégée of John Talbot, the Earl of Shrewsbury, who lived at the mansion known as Alton Towers. Alton Towers resort is set in the grounds of this impressive mansion.

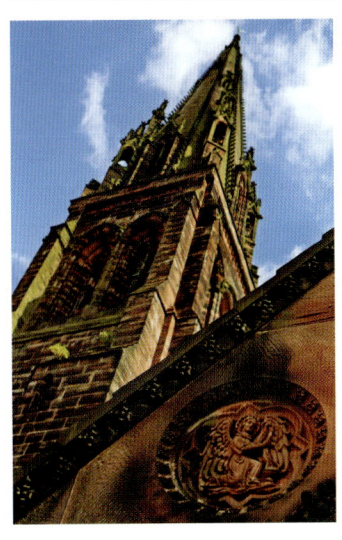

ABOVE: St Giles Catholic Church, Cheadle

ALTON TOWERS

Just a few miles from Cheadle is the fantastic Alton Towers Resort where there's something for everyone, from thrilling white knuckle rides for the more adventurous to the gentle interactive CBeebies Land for the very young. The rides are set in magnificent gardens with a lake. There's a water park too and if you want to take a short break there is a choice of two hotels or woodland lodges and tree houses in the enchanted village.

BIDDULPH

Biddulph Grange Garden

A visit to the National Trust's wonderful garden at Biddulph Grange will take you on a journey of discovery and exploration. Paths, steps and tunnels will guide you through a global journey. Wander round the lake filled with carp, walk through magnificent woodland and find fascinating garden buildings. There is a gift shop, a picnic area and a tea room providing seasonal fare.

This stunning Victorian garden was created by James Bateman, who lived at Biddulph Grange until 1871 when the mansion house was sold to Robert Heath.

Biddulph Grange Country Park

The 73 acre Biddulph Grange Country Park was once part of the Biddulph Grange Estate, which included the mansion house and the surrounding garden now owned by the National Trust.

LEFT: Alton Towers RIGHT: Biddulph Grange

Today the country park has information boards, picnic tables, ponds, a tea room in the visitor centre and several waymarked woodland walks.

A pleasant secluded lake in the park was created in 1903 partly to provide water to fight fires, after a disastrous fire in 1896, which almost destroyed the mansion house. At that time the house and grounds were owned by Robert Heath, a wealthy ironmaster. Nowadays the lake is a haven for water birds, anglers, walkers or anyone who wishes to simply sit and enjoy the scenery.

Greenway Bank Country Park

This picturesque country park just south of Biddulph was formerly part of the Knypersley Hall Estate, once owned by Hugh Henshall the brother in law of the well-known canal engineer, James Brindley. Take a waterside walk around Knypersley Pool or visit the secluded Serpentine Pool; both pools began life as reservoirs. Wander through woodland, meander across lawns and admire the shrubberies which are ablaze with colour during spring and summer.

THE ROACHES

The Roaches with Hen Cloud and Ramshaw Rocks is the name given to a prominent rocky ridge situated above Leek and Tittesworth Reservoir. The ridge with its spectacular rock formations rises to high peaks with majestic views over the countryside. Visitors who follow the waymarked paths are rewarded with breathtaking views and panoramic delights. Whether you are a walker, climber, photographer or a nature lover,

LEFT: The Roaches   RIGHT: Hen Cloud

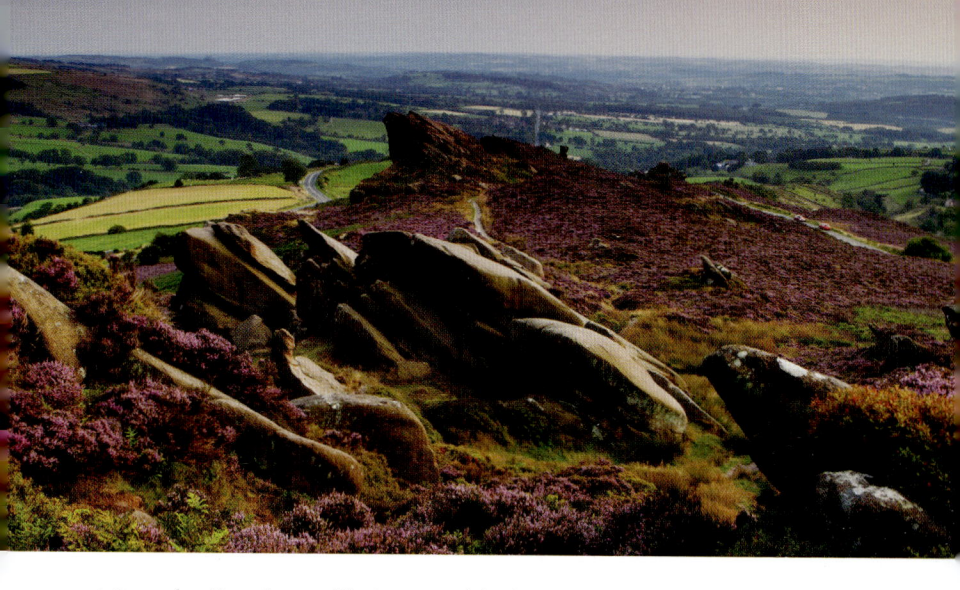

a visit to the Roaches will give untold pleasure. There's a chance to spot buzzards, peregrine falcons, green woodpeckers or red grouse but there's always a lot of sheep! Rock Hall Cottage, partly built into the rocks at the foot of the Roaches, is now a climbing hut but was formerly the home of Doug Moller, the self-styled 'King of the Roaches'. Previously it was the gamekeeper's cottage for the Swythamley estate.

Lud Church

A walk to Lud Church is a revelation, this miniature gorge, with moss and ferns, has its own microclimate. Legends abound in Lud Church and many scholars have identified it as the inspiration for Sir Gawain's Green chapel. Folklore flourishes in the area and myths include the mermaid in the isolated Mermaid (Blakemere) Pool, terrifying nymphs, highwaymen, big cats and ghosts!

ABOVE: Ramshaw Rocks
RIGHT: Lud Church

Tittesworth Water

This reservoir nestles near to the Roaches and is surrounded by spectacular scenery. Bird hides are provided for nature lovers; walkers can stroll along the waterside or tackle a longer walk round the reservoir. There are idyllic picnic areas, a large adventure playground complete with sandpit and a visitor centre with a licensed restaurant and shop. Tittesworth is ideal for a day out for all the family.

Nearby is Tittesworth Water Sports and Activity Centre which offers a range of sporting activities including sport fishing, canoeing, kayaking, sailing and windsurfing. Just a short stroll away is the pretty village of Meerbrook which has a country pub, a church designed by Richard Norman Shaw and an annual scarecrow festival.

Flash

Flash village stands at over 463metres (1,500 feet) above sea level and is the highest village in England. The village was an early centre for Methodism, silk button makers and pedlars. The chapel still stands, now converted into a house, the button makers covered button moulds with silk thread and the pedlars, known as 'Flashmen' hawked ribbons, silk buttons and smallwares around the surrounding countryside.

St Paul's Church stands on land given by the Harpur family who owned vast tracts of land in the area. Their coat of arms can be seen on a window in the church.

Many walks start from Flash including an easy walk from the New Inn, in the village, to the scenic Three Shires Head where, near to the old packhorse bridge, the three counties of Staffordshire, Derbyshire and Cheshire meet.

TOP: Tittesworth Water Sports and Activity Centre   ABOVE: Three Shires Head

Longnor

This former market town stood on a route between London and Buxton. The stable yard can still be seen at The Crewe and Harpur Arms, a former coaching inn, at the bottom of the cobbled Market Place. The Market Hall (1873) still displays a table of tolls for both the sale and purchase of livestock. The quiet lanes and narrow alleys, with their mellow stone buildings, add to the quintessential charm of this delightful village, which in the 19th century was described as being quite as beautiful as Buxton, with invigorating air and striking, romantic scenery. It's still true today! St Bartholomew's Church has a Norman font and a gallery where the Beadle once sat. He kept order among the Sunday school scholars with his long cane by tapping their heads if they fidgeted! Take a walk around this delightful village where you will find an old Methodist chapel, the former blacksmith's premises, interesting inns and the old police house. The Market Hall, now the Craft Centre, is a good place to browse for unusual items or to partake of refreshments before setting off one of the many walks

THE CHURNET VALLEY

Cheddleton

Cheddleton, straddling the A520, boasts an historic flint mill, a Victorian Station and a 13th century church. The Flint Mill, beside the Caldon Canal, once ground flint for the pottery industry. Interpretation boards and enthusiastic volunteer guides help to bring to life the story of the mill. The delightful miller's cottage depicts life in bygone days. A walk or cycle ride along the canal towpath, past the mill, leads to Longsdon, where a stop can be made at Deep Hayes Country Park, before continuing on to The Holly Bush Inn at Denford. This dog friendly, canal side pub, in a picturesque setting, has outside seating areas with narrow boats moored nearby.

ABOVE: Longnor

Back at the Flint Mill a walk in the opposite direction passes under the main road, past the locks to Cheddleton Station and the start of the Churnet Valley Railway line. This charming Victorian station has an excellent tea room together with evocative station buildings. A small museum is located in the former station master's living room.

A train ride along the Churnet Valley takes you on a nostalgic journey through Consall to Froghall and back. The Boat Inn near to Cheddleton station is a pleasant place to enjoy refreshments; the station can be reached by road from the A520, just follow the brown signs along the aptly named Station Road.

The old village of Cheddleton sits at the top of Hollow Lane. The church of St Edward's is a hidden gem where eminent artists and craftsmen have left their mark. Restored by G.G. Scott junior, it has exquisite stained glass by William Morris. Cheddleton certainly has something to offer everyone.

Consall

Consall, downstream from Cheddleton, provides a perfect day out for all the family. Take a picnic, walk the waymarked trails through Consall Nature Park, try a little pond dipping, and look out for birds and butterflies. The park has an interesting visitor centre but is only open on weekend afternoons. Drive or walk down to Consall Forge where the canal and River Churnet converge. Make a stop at the delightful replica Victorian Station before reaching the Black Lion, a traditional canal

TOP LEFT: Churnet Valley looking towards Cheadle   RIGHT: Cheddleton Flint Mill

STAFFORDSHIRE MOORLANDS

side pub with outside sitting areas where you will certainly see boats on the canal and trains on the railway line. Stroll along the towpath a little further to see the restored limekilns, indicative of former bustling industrial activities.

Froghall
The southern terminus of the Churnet Valley Railway is the Kingsley and Froghall Station. The station features a large waiting room, superb Victorian style tea rooms, a booking office and toilets. If you don't want to take the train, it's a good place to simply sit. Just a short distance from the station is Froghall Wharf, once a hive of industrial activity. Now a tranquil area where there are picnic tables, old lime kilns and waymarked walks through the wooded valley.

Alton
A walk round this delightful village will reveal interesting buildings from previous centuries including the roundhouse lockup built in 1819. Dramatically situated Alton Castle now serves as a Catholic Youth Retreat Centre while Pugin's St. John's Catholic Church still serves its original purpose. St Peter's Church has a 13th century tower and a Norman arcade with traces of medieval wall paintings. Enjoy the spectacular surrounding countryside by taking one of the circular walks from the village which will take you through Denstone or Dimminsgdale.

TOP: Consall Forge ABOVE: A day trip on the Churnet Valley Railway

THE MANIFOLD VALLEY

The Manifold Track running from Waterhouses to Hulme End follows the route of the former, narrow gauge, Leek and Manifold Light Railway. It snakes its way through enchanting and varied countryside following the line of the Manifold River. It's perfect for walkers, cyclists and horse riders as the track is surfaced and fairly level along its eight and a half mile length. The track is ideal for families with buggies and for wheelchair users and is car free for most of its length. However, care must be taken if going through the Swainsley Tunnel. A climb up to the imposing Thor's Cave, occupied as long as 10,000 years ago, will be rewarded by panoramic views. Refreshments are available by the river at Wetton Mill and on the site of the old railway station at Hulme End. Cycles can be hired for all the family at Waterhouses where the track begins.

The interesting River Manifold has a neat vanishing trick in the dry season. It disappears underground before Wetton Mill and emerges at the boil holes in the grounds of Ilam Park.

At the end of the Manifold Track at Hulme End linger a while in the Visitor Centre, based in the former ticket office of the Light Railway, where you will find interesting information on the area. Nearby is the Tea Junction, which occupies the refurbished old engine shed. Here you can partake of delicious refreshments in a pleasant setting.

Ilam
The idyllic village of Ilam, in the Staffordshire Peak District, has Swiss style cottages, a Gothic mansion, and an interesting church. The restored cross in the centre of the village is said to be one

TOP: Thor's Cave   ABOVE: Ilam village

STAFFORDSHIRE MOORLANDS

of the finest Gothic revival monuments in the country. Although Ilam Hall is now a Youth Hostel you can explore Ilam Park; enjoy sweeping views, walk through woodland, admire the Italian Garden and discover wildlife on the river banks. Picnic in the spacious grounds; take a break in the charming Manifold Tea Room or browse in the shop. You can easily walk from Ilam Park to nearby Dovedale, both National Trust estates.

Dovedale

Dovedale is renowned for stunning scenery, riverside walks and the famous stepping stones. It has perhaps the most impressive limestone gorge scenery in the country. Popular with families, who can picnic, paddle and play along the banks of the shallow, babbling River Dove. It also attracts hill walkers, botanists, photographers, anglers and climbers. While walking look out for unusual rock formations and caves or be brave enough to climb Thorpe Cloud with rewarding views from the top.

ABOVE: Dovedale

Alstonefield

The chocolate box village of Alstonefield, between the rivers Manifold and Dove, is not far from Dovedale. The village is very popular with tourists as it has an interesting history and is surrounded by a network of paths and tracks. Although no longer a market centre it still has a village green, an Elizabethan manor house, a tithe barn, a 16th century church and a former coaching inn. St Peter's Church is well worth a visit having 17th century box pews and a two-tier pulpit. The richly carved pew of the Cotton family from Beresford Hall has peculiarly been painted a vivid green. After strolling around this delightful village take a walk down to Milldale and the Dove.

FACT FILE

LEEK
Tourist Information Centre
1st Floor
Nicholson Institute
Stockwell Street
Leek
ST13 6DW
Tel. 01538 483741
Email. tourism@staffsmoorlands.gov.uk
www.staffsmoorlands.gov.uk

Brindley's Mill
Mill Street
Leek
ST13 8ET
Sat-Nav to ST13 8FA
Tel. 01538 483741
Email. visit@brindleymill.net
www.brindleymill.net

Foxlowe Arts Centre
Café - Art Gallery – Exhibitions - Music
Market Place
Leek
ST13 6AD
Tel. 01538 386112
Email. hello@foxloweartscentre.org.uk
www.foxloweartscentre.org.uk

The Nicholson Art Gallery and Museum
Stockwell Street
Leek
ST13 6DW
For more information contact The Tourist Information Centre
Tel: 01538 483741
Email. tourism@staffsmoorlands.gov.uk
www.staffordshire.gov.uk/Nicholson

Nicholson War Memorial
www.nicholsonmemorial.org.uk

CHEADLE
Cheadle Discovery and Visitor Centre
Lulworth House
51 High Street
Cheadle
ST10 1AR
Tel. 01538 753519
Email. contact@discovercheadle.co.uk
www.discovercheadle.co.uk/

St Giles Roman Catholic Church
18 Charles Street
Cheadle
ST10 1ED
www.stgilescheadle.org.uk

BIDDULPH
Biddulph Grange Garden
Grange Road
Biddulph
ST8 7SD
Tel. 01782 517999
Email. biddulphgrange@nationaltrust.org.uk
www.nationaltrust.org.uk/biddulph-grange-garden

Biddulph Grange Country Park
Grange Road
Biddulph
Car park ST8 7SB
www.woodlandtrust.org.uk/search

STAFFORDSHIRE MOORLANDS
Alton Towers
Farley Lane
Alton
ST10 4DB
Tel. 0871 222333
www.altontowers.com

Churnet Valley Railway
Kingsley & Froghall Station
Froghall
ST10 2HA
01538 750755
Ticket bookings: 01538 758491
Talking timetable: 01538 758494
Email. enquiries@churnet-valley-railway.co.uk
www.churnet-valley-railway.co.uk

STAFFORDSHIRE MOORLANDS

Cheddleton Flint Mill
Cheadle Road
Cheddleton
ST13 7HL
For opening times, call 0161 408 5083
www.cheddletonflintmill.com

Ilam Park
Ilam
Ashbourne
DE6 2AZ
Tel. 01335 350503
Eamil. peakdistrict@nationaltrust.org.uk
www.nationaltrust.org.uk/ilam-park-dovedale-and-the-white-peak

Brown End Farm Cycle Hire
Leek Road
Waterhouses
ST10 3JR
Tel. 01538 308313
http://www.manifoldcycling-brownendfarm.co.uk

The Manifold Track Cycle Hire Centre
Old Station Car Park
Earlsway
Waterhouses
ST10 3EG
Tel. 01538 308609
Email. davidmvch@gmail.com

Manifold Valley Visitor Centre
Hulme End
Hartington
SK17 0EZ
Tel. 01538 483741

Rudyard Lake
Information Centre the Dam
Lake Road
Rudyard
Leek
ST13 8XB
Tel. 01538 306280
Email. info@Rudyardlake.com
www.rudyardlake.com

Published by Bradwell Books
9 Orgreave Close Sheffield S13 9NP
Email – books@bradwellbooks.co.uk

All rights reserved. No part of this publication may be reproduced, stored in a retrieval system or transmitted in any form or by any means, electronic, mechanical, photocopying, recording or otherwise without the prior permission of Bradwell Books.
A CIP catalogue record for this book is available from the British Library.
1st Edition

ISBN – 9781910551882

Text by: Cathryn Walton
Typeset by: Mark Titterton
Photography: Mark Titterton
Print: Hobbs the Printers Ltd, Totton, Hants

Credits
Additional Photographs: Karl Barton p.2 (top-right) and p.9 (bottom)
© Greg Walker p.2 (bottom)